How to Become a
Software Developer

Start a New Career as a Technical Professional in a Highly In-Demand Field

Table of Contents

Introduction

Choosing a career is probably the hardest decision you will ever have to make in your life. There are a lot of checkboxes every one of us wants to tick off when it comes to the career they want to pursue. Most people want a position that will offer great benefits, flexibility and fulfillment. And, of course, we all want to work in a field that we are interested in and love.

We live in a technology-dependent world that is becoming more digitalized every day. That's why software development is one of the highest in-demand professions around the world. Choosing a career that's in rising demand with an overpoweringly positive outlook has its benefits.

This book will discuss the best parts about being a software developer, the benefits of choosing this as a career path, and explain why this field offers so much. We'll be taking a close look at the different aspects you need to be more aware of in order to grow from a student to a junior developer. If you are tech-savvy and you enjoy being a computer wizard, there is no doubt that software development will help you check all those boxes.

Why Become A Software Developer?

The High Market Demand

Have you ever met a developer that couldn't find a job opportunity that met their needs? This industry has the fastest-growing job opportunities in our technology-driven world. Most companies are desperate to find good talents, and they'd do anything to hire the right professional. Working for a number of local companies will help you develop and fine-tune your skills. Eventually, your chances of getting a position in a top company increase, and you might even find your way to the technology Mekkah of the world; Silicon Valley. SV is the epicenter for developers and people in the tech industry, just like Hollywood is the dream destination for people who want to be in the movie business. Although Silicon Valley might be the end-game for many, it doesn't mean that you can't make it big elsewhere. With the never-ending list of industries that can't reach success without developers, it's guaranteed that you will find several opportunities.

Flexibility

Software developing offers a variety of options that you can choose from. You will have the flexibility to choose your work conditions depending on your needs and likes. You can choose between working for a small company, a large one, or you can go indie and start your own business. Do you want to work in an office with fixed working hours, freelance, or mix and match between the various options? Since you rarely need more than your laptop and a good internet connection, you will be able to work remotely from anywhere in the world. This also offers the added benefit of balancing between work and social life. Working remotely is a rare perk that you will only find in a few careers; you will be able to work whenever you want wherever you want without being suffocated by office rules and politics or struggling with commute. All you need to worry about is getting the job done. Other than that, you can work according to your preferences, regardless of what they are.

High Salary

The demand for this profession is high and is still growing, so it only makes sense that it would offer competitive salaries with awesome benefits. The employment growth percentage between 2014 and 2024 is expected to be 19% or higher; this is more than the average for most livelihoods. Your salary will depend on your skills, the number of languages you know, and how good you are at getting your job done efficiently. Since working remotely is an option, you can choose to work for a richer company abroad that offers higher pay than in your locale. Working in SV can push your salary up to $100k for entry-level positions. The salary in large companies usually ranges around the $120k mark and can go up to $178 when working for companies like Facebook. You can also expect great benefit packages, from financial coaching, a good health insurance plan, life insurance, profit sharing, paid vacations, and the option to work from home when you don't feel like going to the office.

Developing is the Future

Technology has driven many professions to their demise. At the same time, it has opened up and created endless opportunities for software development and other related careers. The future of many industries depends on developers and software engineers. For example, software development offers several benefits for the music industry, including efficient music creation, better accessibility, and production, as well as worldwide exposure. Without coders and developers, many industries would suffer to stay relevant in this interconnected world.

Software Developer Mindsets

The first rule in this never-ending learning journey is embracing your learning curve. You might think that the hardest part is the beginning, but your beginner's mindset allows you to learn fast without the burden of old skills and techniques that you might have to change or re-learn. To maintain that same steep curve, you will have to realize that there will always be room for improvement, new skills to develop, and things to learn. Your passion for knowledge is one of the few constant key ingredients to becoming successful in any profession. In software development, your mindset is your asset; having the right one is guaranteed to pay off in the end, whether in terms of personal and professional fulfillment, intellectually, and even philosophically. Your whole thinking process will take a new turn, and this ultimately has the power to make both your professional and personal life a lot easier.

Different Mindsets to Acquire

After you start learning more in this field, you might face a developer's block where you get stuck. You will feel like you are not making any progress at all, coupled with overwhelming feelings of frustration that might start hitting you hard. Experts have proven that the mindset of a learner, a programmer, and a crafter are the main three mindsets that will prevent the block from happening. The cornerstones of having a learner's mindset are not only accepting that you will make mistakes but to also embrace and learn from them. You might think you are wasting your time, but your willingness to experiment with concepts you are not familiar with yet and writing codes that will test your boundaries will give you answers to many unanswered questions. You have to realize that your improvement will not always be linear. If you acquire these concepts, you will easily avoid problems like procrastinating, frustration and giving up. The programmer's mindset depends on mastering these three aspects in this particular order.

1. You need to start with reading and understanding code. At first, you might think that the alphabetical arrangement with different letters, numbers, and punctuation marks don't make any sense. If you compare coding to our common language, it will never make sense to you. It's a different language used to communicate with the computer and give it instructions. Keeping that in mind will make the next steps easier.

2. Accuracy and attending to details are the thin line between a bad programmer and a good one. Even if you think that you are not naturally attentive to details, you can easily start acquiring this critical skill. Machines will not understand what you want to say if you don't write the code with 100% accuracy. The misplacement of a simple semicolon can be the reason why your code isn't working. That's why you need extreme focus and attention when coding, especially in the beginning. It's also a must to go over your work several times.

3. Always find a way. If you can't, create one. Nowadays, learning any new set of skills has

become a lot easier than before. With a click of a button, you will have all the answers to your questions. Whether you're stuck or just need a little extra help, you will find books, online forums for programmers, blogs and articles, online tutors and more to help give you that extra push. With all these available resources we have access to, giving up shouldn't be an option.

The hardest, yet most rewarding, part of learning any new skill is the ability to keep practicing. You don't have to practice all day every day. All you need is a bulletproof schedule that you can stick to. Throughout the day, keep an eye on your energy levels. Notice the times when your focus is optimum, and your ability to learn or work are prime. This trick helps you figure out the golden hours when you tend to be at your highest productivity levels. Are you an early bird or a night owl? Do your energy levels dip in the afternoon, and would probably be best reserved for mundane tasks or even a nap? If you make a habit out of practicing at a specific hour every day, your brain will program itself to automatically focus all its attention on what you're doing.

Mastering the Fundamentals

There are a few fundamental laws for software development. If you master these, you will be able to prevent small yet common issues that most developers run into.

- Problem Solving

While many people despise Math, some are fascinated by its equations and problems; they find joy in solving and tackling these problems. Think of any obstacle you run into as an equation that you are trying to solve. You will realize that there is a set of rules that can help you overcome any problem you might face in your career or personal life. First, you have to identify the problem and understand it; if you don't understand it, you won't be able to solve it. Your second step should be brainstorming and planning the different ways you can use to solve this problem. After finding the best solution for your errors and bugs, you can proceed with the solution. This process is all about trial and error while having enough patience to solve for X.

- Creativity

Think of yourself as an artist. Having a crafter's mindset is what will make your journey joyful and interesting. There is no rule that software development should be the only thing you enjoy in life. However, if you learn how to creatively use your designer's mindset, you will fall in love with your work. Your work depends on finding creative solutions and thinking outside the box in order to excel.

- Simplicity Over Complexity

Brian Kernighan, the famous Canadian computer scientist, once said: *"Controlling complexity is the essence of computer programming."* Expanding software purposes will inevitably lead to complexity and doom your project to failure. The ability to produce a simple code is what sets a good designer and a bad one apart. If you focus on reducing the complexity as much as you can, you will be able to execute good working software. Even clearing out bugs and errors will be a piece of cake.

- The Ability To Keep Learning

As someone whose work is based on technology, you have to accept that you will spend your whole life learning. If you think about it, this is definitely a good thing. You will not feel stuck in a systematic job for the rest of your life where you do the same thing over and over again. Technology changes and evolves at a fast pace, and you have to learn how to keep up with all the new changes that pop up.

How to Learn a Programming Language

Most people get hung up on choosing the first programming language they need to learn. It's a mistake to overwhelm oneself with the burden of learning all the languages that exist. Once you learn two or three languages, it will be easy to pick up on the differences between them in case your job demands that you use a language that you didn't learn.

As a beginner, deciding on which language to start with depends on different questions that you need to answer. Do you want to start with the easiest one? Python, HTML, and Java are considered to be relatively easy languages anyone can learn. Do you want to learn a language that will help you with acquiring other languages? Logically the answer would be C. Even though this language is harder and trickier to comprehend, it will ultimately open doors for learning other languages easily such as C++ and C#. On the other hand, if you want to focus on market needs, then JavaScript is your answer. It's extremely popular and is currently considered to be the highest sought-after programming language.

It's best to take your time while making this decision. Specify your priorities and do your research before you settle on the language you want to start with. Once you do, stick to your choice. Why? Because stopping in the middle, giving up, or jumping to another language will do more harm than good. The essence of learning any new programming language can be summed up in a few steps that can be easily followed to guarantee success.

The Starter Pack

Reading codes even if you don't understand them will benefit you greatly in terms of understanding the basics and getting familiar with how they look. The more you read, the sooner codes will start making sense to you. Beginning your learning journey with understanding the basics of programming and algorithms is recommended. It's also advisable to get comfortable enough with the language before starting with the framework. Learning the framework without mastering the language can create a lot of issues that beginners are better off without.

Online Resources

Before committing to courses in real life or deciding to sign up for programming classes or degrees, it's best to make use of the endless online resources first. This tip is especially important for people who don't have any programming background. Online courses will ease you into the world of codes. This way, you will be able to understand all the basics you need to learn before proceeding with learning the complicated technical lessons. Online courses have many other benefits, even for experienced programmers. All you need to do is find the courses that match your level of knowledge while offering the same targets you are trying to reach. Learning online from the comfort of one's home can make new students less nervous about their level of programming. You can find many options that will offer different courses for free, and some courses will only charge you for certification.

Other than that, you can learn all you want without paying a penny.

Practice and Experiment

Testing out the things you have learned practically is the only way you will be able to master any language. In the beginning, you might run into a lot of bugs or be frustrated with the fact that you're a slow coder. That's completely fine. Embracing the learning curve and giving yourself some time for your hard work to start paying off will keep you motivated enough to continue the journey.

Helpful Tools

There are some code-analyzer tools – linters - that can be used to point out bugs, idiomatic misses, style errors, and offer other helpful tips. Using these tools, in the beginning, will help you execute a polished code faster and with little frustration. Pointing out errors and bugs will ease up the process of solving and clearing them out. That's why the linting tool shouldn't be overlooked.

Resume Tips

There is a huge difference between writing a technical report and writing a resume. The art of writing resumes depends on the ability to execute a well-rounded one that will not only draw the attention of recruiters but will convince them to give you the job. Your resume needs to stand out from hundreds of others that are applying for the same position. It's your chance to make a good first impression. There are some common mistakes you can easily avoid and will make a world of difference when you finally send that resume in. Fatal mistakes can deny you your dream job; that's how powerful CVs are.

Software Developer Resume Formats

Recruiters usually take quick glances at the applied candidates' resumes to create a shortlist of the eligible ones. To make it into the shortlist, your CV must be clear, pleasing, and well-formatted. There are three types of the most eye-catching and professional formats. Chronological resumes focus on telling a story about the developer's past, present, and where they are willing to go in the future. A functional resume is geared more towards shedding light on your abilities, skills, and achievements. The third type is a combination of both.

Try your best to not just create another generic resume. Instead, organize the CV with a side column to list the different sections in your resume while going bold for headlines; you can also use different dark colors for headlines and the body, such as dark blue and black. The ideal resume should have enough heading sections to cover all the required information for any job post. Here are the six main headlines you need to start with:

- A summary of your vision, what you can bring to the table, and what you are looking for, along with a few details about you such as your name, date of birth, and your preferred method of communication.
- Work Experience.
- Skills.
- Education and all the courses you have completed.

- Certificates.

- Languages you can speak, programming languages, and software or technology programs.

Enhance Your Resume with Clickable Links

Adding hyperlinks to your other profiles such as LinkedIn, Upwork (or other freelancing websites you have active profiles on), and a link to your GitHub account will give recruiters a chance to know more about you and the value you can add to their company. You can also make use of this chance and add other hyperlinks for any work that you have completed, or a link to your portfolio. It's impossible to resist clicking on hyperlinks. So, make sure that you use this feature to show off your work and what you can do. This way, you will guarantee a phone interview or an acceptance email by the time they are done reading your resume.

Mistakes to Be Avoided

- Don't use the same resume for different job posts.
- Don't focus on technical skills and disregard the emotional and mental skills. For example, don't forget to add skills such as emotional intelligence, team player, communication skills, interpersonal skills, and others.
- Lying about your level of knowledge will do more harm than good.

Getting Through the Interview

Mental Preparation

Once you're ready, applying for jobs is the next natural step. You may have gone through interviews before in different fields, but there are some differences you need to be aware of when interviewing for a software developer position. A software developer's interview is technical, and these are a bit more stressful than non-technical ones. You don't need to feel like this is a test that you have to ace by making absolutely zero mistakes; some mistakes are acceptable as long as they are not fatal. If you let a few questions take you off-guard and stress you out to the point that you start forgetting everything you have learned, you might end up losing the battles and the war. The one thing you need to keep in mind is that not getting the job isn't the end of the world. Remember, this is a high-demand job, and companies are always looking. Keeping your spirit high and persisting ensures that you will eventually get the dream job you're looking for.

Practice Makes Perfect

The difference between a software developer's interview and an academic test is that, in an interview, you're being assessed on more than just your ability to solve specific problems. Knowing the approaches that you will choose is the main target behind most of the questions asked.

- The best way to prepare yourself is by beefing up your problem-solving skills through practice. Practicing will eventually enable you to solve any problem, even the unfamiliar ones that you have never run into.
- Find the perfect strategy that suits you.
- Never rush to coding before you've thought out a thorough plan.

Aside from honing your problem-solving skills, you should also practice the art of interviewing. You can perform mock interviews and start preparing for the non-technical part of the interview. If you have the time, try going to as many interviews as you possibly can. Even if they are not in the job position you are after, they will help you get a feel of what to expect. Also, not caring enough about the interviews you are going to have to practice your skills and this might give you a confidence boost that will make it easier for you to land these positions. It never hurts to have a backup plan in case anything goes wrong.

Stay Composed

You need to know that being nervous never helps. Sure, it's easier said than done, but it does have to be said nevertheless. It's recommended to stay relaxed and calm to be able to ace an interview. Professionalism and confidence are often associated with a composed and calm demeanor.

- Make sure you've researched the company you're applying to. This will show that you care enough to do your homework. It will also show that you are interested in the company.

- Be punctual. Don't just arrive right on time, but try to be there early. If you are in a rush, you won't have the time to relax and collect your thoughts.
- Don't linger in negativity. Stay focused on your strongest suits and keep reassuring yourself that you are the right person for the job.
- Fake it until you make it doesn't always work; confidence doesn't suddenly appear out of thin air. You have to believe in yourself for other people to believe in you.
- Speak about your tech passions. This will greatly work in your favor as it will show that this isn't just a job to you.

Preparing for Questions

Employers usually look for candidates who can add value to their roles and help the company grow. Understanding this will make predicting the questions a lot easier. It's common for interviewers to ask you about a tough previous problem you've encountered and how you've managed to solve it. They're looking to see if you're able to demonstrate your teamwork and coding skills in synchronization. Any team-based job has conflict, which is why employers usually want to know how you, as a potential employee, will approach such conflicts. Your interpersonal skills and ability to work with others are two of the most important focal points in any team-based job. To be able to truly prepare for the questions, you can check previous experiences with interviews in the company you are going to. Websites such as Glassdoor, for example, allow current and former employees to post their interview and overall work experiences in different companies. This could be extremely helpful to not only prepare your answers but to understand more about the mentality of the company and how you should deal with it.

Projects

In some interviews, you may be asked to either showcase your coding skills by writing code, present one of your projects, or both. It's recommended to get yourself a GitHub account where you can keep track of your projects and contributions, all in one place. A few project examples can help increase your chances of getting hired. Passion projects are also one of the strongest indicators of good developers. Working on personal projects can truly show that you care for the field while also showing your constant effort to improve your skills. This can give you conversation points that could showcase your interest in the position you're applying for.

Former Employers

Questions about your former employers are very common in all interviews. Whatever the reason is for your need to change companies or fields of expertise, your employer shouldn't get the impression that you're unpredictable. It's normal for your potential employer to want to know what they can expect from you and how you choose to approach issues. It's recommended you don't badmouth your previous employers. Instead, try to showcase diplomatic skills by outlining the critical points where you may have not met eye-to-eye with your previous employer. Showing that you are level-headed and straightforward is very important when it comes to leaving a good impression.

Tips for the First Few Months on the Job

Software developers often handle the building of infrastructure, lessen security breaches, implement designs, write detailed technical reports, or help in building data storage solutions. Your job might consist of one of these requirements, two, or all of the above; it depends on your position. The first few months in any job can feel very overwhelming and confusing, yet there is an excitement about landing a good opportunity that allows you to practice what you have been patiently learning. Here are some vital tips to help you ace your first few months and prove to your employers that they made the right choice.

Knowledge Gaps Are Normal

All the books you've read and courses you've taken are essential to teaching you the important basics of how to code and arming you with the required skills. Yet, books seldom prepare you for the real world. Even if you have work experience from previous job positions, handling work in a new company will definitely differ tremendously. Software development is so much more than just knowing how to code. That's why it's ok to accept that you might have some gaps in your knowledge that you will need to work on. Here are some examples:

- Learning about diversely used technologies for different problems.
- How to read and understand other people's codes.
- Understanding different practices and design patterns.
- Testing codes.
- Learning how to be a team player. You need to have an open mind and patience to work with other developers, clients, teams, and management.

Accepting that you might not know everything you need to in the first few months is the number one step to overcoming the overwhelming feelings of inadequacy and frustration. Constantly teaching yourself new skills and keeping up with changes are the cornerstones in this career choice; always learning new things is part of its beauty.

Never Be Too Shy To Ask

There is no shame in asking questions and requesting help when you are stuck. The most important part of being a successful software developer is asking the right questions. Your manager and team members are there to support you. The common reasons behind the fear of asking questions lie in the fears of being a burden, showing vulnerability, or being afraid of getting mocked. To overcome those feelings, you have to realize that they are only in your head. People respect others who are courageous enough to admit that they don't know. On the other hand, you have to realize that you are not forcing anyone to answer your questions; practical people tend to offer help if they have some time to spare. If they don't, they will simply let you know.

Accept Criticism

It's called constructive criticism for a reason. Reviews are a coder's best friends; they help you grow as a developer. Reviews give you the chance to learn from your mistakes and find new ways to avoid repeating them. Your first review might feel devastating, but the smart thing to do is to not doubt yourself as a developer. Viewing feedback as a statement of how bad you are will only drive you to give up. Feedback is there to help you improve and learn; that's why you should welcome and expect them. Your turn will come when you get a chance to help other people by reviewing their codes. You will learn how fulfilling it is for team members to help each other.

Always Break Down Problems and Tasks

If you feel overwhelmed by any of your tasks or the problems that you will be subjected to, it's always easier to break them down. Questions such as when to start, how to start, which path to take, or any other confusing questions will inevitably pop up. The smart thing to do is to break down your tasks and problems into smaller ones. This way you will be able to understand them and search for solutions without being burdened by overthinking. Once you've found solutions to the various small problems, the only thing left to do is connect the dots. Then you can review the bigger picture until it makes sense to you.

Conclusion

If there's one skill set that's making its way through the ranks of importance and priority in the world of today, it's software development. Programming and software engineering are the basis for almost every industry and business. Without those, many industries will suffer. They will never be able to reach the top, and they can say goodbye to efficiency. From building spaceships to analyzing statistics, software is embedded in the fabric of technological progress. It's considered the benchmark of how a successful technology-related field is doing in the market.

Software developers are indispensable to the IT community. There are multiple paths to becoming a successful developer. While these paths may differ, sometimes they cross and share the same common concepts.

While this book outlines what this field has to offer and how to carve the appropriate approach to becoming a software developer, it must all be driven by one's own motivation for success and thirst for knowledge. Becoming a software developer requires adapting to traditional job responsibilities while staying connected to the deep pulse of the technological world. The challenges faced by software developers are mainly byproducts of a fast-paced field that will always be growing and evolving. Our main job as developers lies in catching up with this speeding train and adding our own touch to the journey.

www.ingramcontent.com/pod-product-compliance
Lightning Source LLC
Chambersburg PA
CBHW031549080326
40690CB00055B/1022